Student Response Book

Summer Success® Reading

James F. Baumann • Michael F. Opitz • Laura Robb

GReaT SouRCe®
EDUCATION GROUP
A Houghton Mifflin Company

Credits

Editorial: Alex Culpepper/Judy Bernheim

Writer: Anina Robb

Design/Production: Jim Bartosik/Andy Cox, David Drury

Illustration: Chris Vallo and Jim Higgins

Poetry credits: "Winter Wraps" by Carol E. Reed-Jones from *Once Upon Ice and Other Frozen Poems,* copyright © 1997. "Fog" by Carl Sandburg from *Chicago Poems* by Carl Sandburg. Copyright 1916 by Holt, Rhinehart and Winston, Inc., renewed 1944 by Carl Sandburg, reprinted by permission of Harcourt, Inc. "Wouldn't You Think?" text copyright © 2001 by Aileen Fisher from *Sing of the Earth and Sky: Poems about Our Planet and the Wonders Beyond* by Aileen Fisher. Published by Wordsong/Boyds Mills Press, Inc. Reprinted by permission. "If I can stop one heart from breaking." Reprinted by permission of the publishers and the Trustees of Amherst College from *The Poems of Emily Dickinson,* Thomas H. Johnson, ed., Cambridge, Mass.: The Belknap Press of Harvard University Press, Copyright © 1951, 1955, 1979 by the President and Fellows of Harvard College. "Long Trip" from *The Collected Poems of Langston Hughes* by Langston Hughes, copyright © 1994 by The Estate of Langston Hughes. Used by permission of Alfred A. Knopf, a division of Random House, Inc. "What is it that upsets the volcanoes," by Pablo Neruda, translated by William O'Daly, from *The Book of Questions,* copyright © 1991.

Copyright © 2002 by Great Source Education Group, Inc. All rights reserved.

Permission is hereby granted to teachers who have purchased a *Summer Success*®: *Reading* kit (ISBN 0-669-49160-8) to reprint or photocopy in classroom quantities the pages or sheets in this work that carry a copyright notice, provided each copy made shows the copyright notice. Such copies may not be sold and further distribution is expressly prohibited. Except as authorized above, prior written permission must be obtained from Great Source Education Group, Inc., to reproduce or transmit this work or portions thereof in any other form or by any other electronic or mechanical means, including any information storage or retrieval system, unless expressly permitted by federal copyright law. Address inquiries to Great Source Education Group, Inc., 181 Ballardvale Street, Wilmington, Massachusetts 01887.

Great Source® and *Summer Success*® are registered trademarks of Houghton Mifflin Company.

Printed in the United States of America

International Standard Book Number: 0-669-49164-0

1 2 3 4 5 6 7 8 9 10 - MZ - 07 06 05 04 03 02

Name _____ Date _____

Questions Good Readers Ask Themselves

Making Connections
- What do I know about the topic of a selection?
- What does this selection remind me of?
- What would I do if I were the main character?
- Has the selection changed how I think?

Understanding Text Structure
- What text structure(s) does the author use: descriptive, listing, cause/effect, time-order (chronological), problem/solution, compare/contrast?
- How can I use the text structure to organize and remember information?

Monitoring Understanding
- Does what I am reading make sense?
- If I don't understand something, what can I do?
- How can I figure out an unfamiliar word?

Visualizing
- What picture do I see in my mind?
- What connections can I make from the picture to my life?

Retelling/Summarizing
- What happened in this story? What were the main events?
- What was this selection mainly about? What were the main ideas?
- What was new or surprising in the selection?
- Would I recommend the selection to a friend? Why?

Name _____   Date _____

Reading Log Questions

Choose one question to answer for each selection (article, story, or book) that you write about in the Reading Log.

1. What did this selection remind you of?
2. What did you learn that was new or interesting?
3. What was this selection mainly about?
4. What questions do you have for the author?
5. How is the main character like you?

Reading Log

Title _____

Question # _____

_____

_____

_____

_____

Title _____

Question # _____

_____

_____

_____

_____

Name _____ Date _____

READING LOG

Title _____

Question # _____

_____
_____
_____
_____

Title _____

Question # _____

_____
_____
_____
_____

Title _____

Question # _____

_____
_____
_____
_____

Name _____ Date _____

READING LOG

Title _____

Question # _____

_____
_____
_____
_____
_____

Title _____

Question # _____

_____
_____
_____
_____
_____

Title _____

Question # _____

_____
_____
_____
_____
_____

Name _____ Date _____

What Good Readers Do to Read Words

Look at the whole word
- Look at the beginning, middle, and end of the word.
- Say the word in parts or syllables.
- Think of a word that looks similar.

Examine word parts
- Look for any prefixes or suffixes.
- Look for a root word that you recognize, and think of its meaning.
- Look for a familiar spelling pattern.

Use context
- Read to the end of a sentence to find clues to meaning.
- Read the sentences before the word to look for clues to meaning.
- Read the sentences after the word to look for clues to meaning.
- Think about the plot or main idea to see if that offers clues to meaning.

Use resources
- Ask for help.
- Look in a dictionary.
- Look for the word in other books.

Name _____   Date _____

Word Bank

Week 1
_____
_____
_____
_____
_____

Week 2
_____
_____
_____
_____
_____

Week 3
_____
_____
_____
_____
_____

Week 4
_____
_____
_____
_____
_____

Week 5
_____
_____
_____
_____
_____

Week 6
_____
_____
_____
_____
_____

Summer Success®: Reading

© Great Source. Permission is granted to copy this page.

Name _____ Date _____

Reading Strategies Survey

1 **Before I read a book, I usually do these things:**

(Check any of the following strategies that you use.)

_____ ask someone what it's about
_____ look at the pictures
_____ look to see if it's too hard
_____ look to see if it's too easy
_____ guess what it's about
_____ read the back cover or the jacket flap

2 **When I'm reading and I don't understand what's happening,**

I usually try to _____
_____.

Here's an example of what I did once: _____
_____.

3 **When I get stuck on a word, I usually do these things:**

(Check any of the following strategies that you use.)

_____ ask someone
_____ skip it and read on
_____ read the whole part again
_____ try to sound it out
_____ look it up
_____ think of a word that makes sense

4 **After I finish a book I liked a lot, I usually do these things:**

(Check anything you do.)

_____ talk to a friend about it
_____ look for another by the same author
_____ read the book again
_____ take a rest from reading
_____ choose a new book
_____ think of how it was like my life
_____ ask someone to suggest another book
_____ draw or write about it

Summer Success®: Reading

Name _____   Date _____

Reading Interest Survey

Put a ✓ in the spaces to show your answers.

1 Do you like to read?

_____ yes   _____ sometimes   _____ no

2 What kinds of books do you like to read? Mark all the ones you like.

_____ realistic fiction   _____ horror stories

_____ science fiction   _____ mystery

_____ historical fiction   _____ humor

_____ poems   _____ fantasy

_____ riddles/jokes   _____ series

3 What is your favorite book? _____
_____

4 Who is your favorite author? _____
_____

5 What magazines do you like to read? _____
_____

6 When and where do you read? _____
_____

7 How do you choose books to read? _____
_____

Dear Parent or Caregiver,

This summer, your son or daughter will be using the **Summer Success: Reading** program. This program will provide instruction in reading skills and strategies to help him or her read better. **Summer Success: Reading** features different types of reading (fiction, nonfiction, poetry) and topics. Each week, your son or daughter will bring home a weekly newsletter so you will be able to keep in touch with his or her activities in summer school.

Summer Success: Reading emphasizes reading strategies. This means that the program has instruction in helping your son or daughter understand what he or she is reading. One example of a strategy is "making connections." A reader who makes connections asks questions like "What do I know about this?" "What does this remind me of?" "How am I like this character?" When a reader can make connections, he or she understands the text.

Summer Success: Reading also works with words, helping your son or daughter become better at reading and writing words. A section of the lesson called Read & Explore Words focuses on how words work. Students will study words, make words from letters, classify words, and—in general—get to know words.

But we cannot do it alone at school. We need your help as well. On the back of this letter are things you can do at home to support the summer school program. Doing reading and writing activities every day will help your son or daughter develop his or her reading ability this summer and beyond. Please let me know if you have any questions. Thank you.

Educationally yours,

Your son or daughter's teacher

© Great Source. Permission is granted to copy this page.

Summer Success®: Reading

Read, Read, Read!

The more you read with your son or daughter, the more opportunities he or she will have to enjoy reading and improve reading skills. Try to have a variety of books at home. If you don't know what books to get, ask other children what they like to read. Librarians, bookstore workers, and teachers are good resources, too.

Make sure your son or daughter reads every day.

- Provide access to a variety of books.
- Share what you are reading.
- Ask about what your son or daughter is reading.

Model how to think about the text. Say things like,

"This reminds me of _____."
"I wonder why _____."
"I predict that _____."
"I would like to ask the author _____."

When your son or daughter has free time, try one of these ideas.

- Read a book.
- Read a magazine or newspaper.
- Read a recipe and cook something.
- Make up a play with a friend.
- Write a story.
- Write a letter.

Winter Wraps

by Carol E. Reed-Jones

Winter wraps
a brittle cape of cold
around a rock
and buttons it
with
a
single
leaf.

1 When writers give human qualities and traits to objects or animals, they are using personification. What human ability does winter have in this poem?
_____
_____
_____

2 How does this poem make you feel?
_____
_____
_____

Week 1

Name _____ Date _____

Before You Read

Fill in the K-W-L chart.

1. Write all that you know about winter sports in the *K* column.
2. Write what you want to know in the *W* column. You will fill in the *L* column later.
3. Share with a partner what you know and what you want to know.

K What I Know	W What I Want to Know	L What I Learned

Summer Success®: Reading

Week 1

Name _____ Date _____

Make the Connection

Do you ever say to yourself as you read, "What would I do in this character's situation?" When you think like this, you are making a connection to the story.

1 As you read the story "The Last Practice" on pages 4–5 of the *Winter Sports* magazine, underline parts of the story that make connections with your feelings or experiences.

2 Record your connections in the chart below.

Connections to Characters	Connections to Settings

Connections to Events/Actions	Connections to Other Features

Is there anything in the story that you couldn't make a connection to or that surprised you? Explain. _____

Summer Success®: Reading

Week 1

Name _____ Date _____

Three Is a Crowd!

The prefix *tri-* means "three." When you add the prefix *tri-* to a root, it changes the root's meaning. Example: *tri-* + *athletes* = *triathletes*. A triathlete is a person in a competition that includes three sporting events.

Work with a partner, and make a list of words that use the prefix *tri-*. Write the words in the space provided.

SCRAMBLED SYLLABLES: Rearrange each of the following syllable groups to create a multi-syllable word. Notice that each group contains one extra syllable!

EXAMPLE:

lar u ang tri par = triangular

1. pod tri for
2. ceps tri pos
3. co lor tri ic
4. lon tri ath sto
5. cle tri cy so
6. sect of tri
7. cho dent tri
8. an gle do tri

CHALLENGE: With your partner, try to figure out the meanings of the starred words above. Remember that the prefix *tri-* means "three." Write the word and your prediction of its definition. Then check the meaning of the word by looking in a dictionary.

Word	My Prediction	Dictionary Meaning

Summer Success®: Reading

Week 1

Name _____ Date _____

Take Note

Read the article "Get Going in the Snow" on pages 6–9 of the *Winter Sports* magazine. Pay attention to the new details you learn about different winter sports.

1 In the box provided, write the name of one of the winter sports you read about.

2 Sketch something you would use to participate in the sport.

3 Then, complete the chart by telling what you learned about the sport. You might need to reread the article.

Winter Sport

Name of Sport _____

My Sketch

What I Learned About It _____
_____
_____

Using your notes from the chart, describe what it would be like to participate in the sport you learned about.
_____
_____

Summer Success®: Reading

Week 1

Name _____ Date _____

Question It!

Preview "The Last Great Race" on pages 10–12 of the *Winter Sports* magazine. Look at the pictures and read the subheads, the first and last sentences, and the boldfaced words.

1 In the Questions column in the chart below, list questions that come to your mind as you preview and read the article. Tip: You can turn subheads into questions.

2 Record your answers in the Answers column.

Questions	Answers

18 Summer Success®: Reading

Week 1

Name _____ Date _____

"Not" This!

A prefix is a word part that can be added to the beginning of a root word to change the meaning of the word. Some prefixes have similar meanings. For example, *dis-*, *in-*, *non-*, and *un-* all mean "not" and change a word into an opposite. Complete sentences 1–6 with a phrase that fits.

Dis- I *disagree* with you. = I *do not agree* with you.

In- The loud noise was *intolerable*. = The loud noise was *not tolerable*.

Non- That idea is *nonsense*. = That idea *does not make sense*.

Un- Eating too many chips is *unhealthy*. = Eating too many chips is *not healthy*.

1. Some parents often want their children to watch **noncommercial** television because _____.

2. A student who hands in an **incomplete** paper _____.

3. If you are **uncertain** of the answer to a test question, _____.

4. Something that might cause **discomfort** _____.

5. If you are **unaware** of the schedule for the day, _____.

6. Someone who is **dishonest** _____.

List several other words that begin with these prefixes.

dis-	*non-*
in-	*un-*

Summer Success®: Reading

Week 1

Name _____ Date _____

Get Ready to Write

Get ready to write an informative paragraph about how to survive when you are lost during the winter.

A. Gather Ideas

Write a list of ideas from "Winter Survival Guide" on pages 13–14 of the *Winter Sports* magazine that tell how to survive in the winter. Put a star next to the three most important details, which you will include in your paragraph. Then number the details in the order in which you will include them.

SURVIVOR

B. Plan Your Paragraph

1. Complete the topic sentence.
2. Draft a closing sentence that tells how you feel about your topic.

Topic Sentence: If you know what to do, you can _____.

Closing Sentence: _____

20 Summer Success®: Reading

Time to Write

You are ready to write your own paragraph.

1. Open with your topic sentence.
2. Use the three details you listed on page 20 in complete sentences to support your topic sentence.
3. Finish your paragraph with your closing sentence.
4. Remember to give your paragraph a title.

Title: _____

Week 1

Name _____ Date _____

Self-Evaluation

1 What are three new facts that you learned from the *Winter Sports* magazine?
_____
_____
_____

2 What part of the magazine did you most enjoy reading? Why?
_____
_____
_____

3 What are two new words you learned this week? Use each one in a sentence.

Word	Sentence Using the Word
_____	_____
	_____
_____	_____
	_____

4 What strategy do you use most when you read? How does it help you?
_____
_____

5 What is one goal you have for next week? How will you reach it?
_____
_____
_____

22 Summer Success®: Reading

Take It Home!

Word Challenge

Scramble letters in the word *triathletes* to make new words. Write your words on the lines below.

Give yourself 1 point for each one-syllable word.

Give yourself 2 points for each two-syllable word.

Give yourself 3 points for each three-syllable word.

One has been done to get you started.

New Words	Points I Get
leather	2

_____ **Total Points**

Write a Letter

Now that you know more about winter sports, write a letter to a friend and tell him or her about a winter sport that you would like to try. Use the web below to organize your ideas before you write.

- What I like about this sport
- What I wonder about this sport
- My Sport
- What would be most difficult about this sport
- How I can get involved in this sport

WRITE AWAY: Write your letter on the lines below. Include some of the ideas you listed in the word web.

Dear _____,

I've been learning about winter sports this week, and the one I'd most like to try is _____

_____

_____

_____

Your Friend,

_____

24 Summer Success®: Reading

Week 1 Newsletter

This week we read about different winter sports. We listened to a story read aloud, and we read some magazine articles and poems. Take a moment to ask your son or daughter to tell you about the book that was read aloud. Also ask what he or she learned from reading and thinking about the *Winter Sports* magazine.

The word of the week was *triathletes.* With partners, the students used the prefix *tri-* to create words. Using what they learned about the prefix *tri-,* they predicted the meanings of words. We learned that several prefixes have the same meaning. *Dis-, non-, in-,* and *un-* all add the meaning "not" or "opposite of" to a word. Prefixes are important because they can be used to help determine the meaning of an unfamiliar word.

Here is what your son or daughter has to say about the week:

_____
_____
_____
_____
_____
_____
_____
_____
_____
_____
_____
_____

Week 1 Newsletter

The best way to become better at something is to practice. Practice is important in sporting events as well as in reading. Listed below are several books that continue the topic of winter sports that your son or daughter explored this week. Encourage your son or daughter to read by providing suggestions of books that meet his or her interest and reading ease. For more suggestions, talk to your local librarian or try the Book Adventure Web site (http://www.bookadventure.org/).

***Adventure in Alaska* by S. A. Kramer (Random House, 1993)** Libby Riddles was the first woman to win the Iditarod. Read about her incredible race to the finish past hungry wolves and killer moose, through howling wind and subfreezing temperatures.

***Dogsong* by Gary Paulsen (Simon & Schuster, 1995)** Fifteen-year-old Russell travels with a dog team across ice floes, tundras, and mountains in search of himself. Along the way, he has a vision inspired by an Eskimo shaman, which helps him save the life of a young girl. A Newbery winner.

***Ice Warrior* by Ruth Riddell (Simon & Schuster, 1992)** When his mom remarries, twelve-year-old Rob is forced to move from sunny California to Minnesota. He feels as though he doesn't belong until he discovers iceboating, which he hopes will help him gain the respect of his peers. Above all, he wants to win a trophy to prove himself to his highly competitive father.

Fog

by Carl Sandburg

The fog comes
on little cat feet.

It sits looking
over harbor and city
on silent haunches
and then moves on.

Metaphor

Poems can surprise you with unexpected ideas. One way poets do this is through the use of metaphor. A metaphor compares one object to another without using a comparison word such as *like* or *as*. Carl Sandburg compares fog to a cat; he describes the fog as a cat.

1 What does the phrase "the fog comes on little cat feet" tell you about the fog?

_____
_____

2 What do you picture when you read the second stanza?

_____
_____

3 What else could fog be compared to? Why?

_____
_____

Week 2

Name _____ Date _____

Before You Read

Previewing what you read can help you make connections with it. Look through the *Boats and Boating* magazine.

❶ Read the introduction on page 3.

❷ Read the titles of the selections in the magazine.

❸ Look at the pictures and other features.

❹ When you've finished, answer the questions below.

1. What do you think you are going to learn from this magazine?

   _____
   _____
   _____

2. What kinds of connections do you think you will be able to make with this magazine?

   _____
   _____
   _____

3. What questions do you have about boats and boating?

   _____
   _____
   _____

Week 2

Name _____ Date _____

Asking Questions

1 Read the article "The Art of Sailing" on pages 4–6 of the *Boats and Boating* magazine.

2 Turn three of the headings into questions. Look for answers to your questions as you read each section.

3 Write your questions and answers in the sails below.

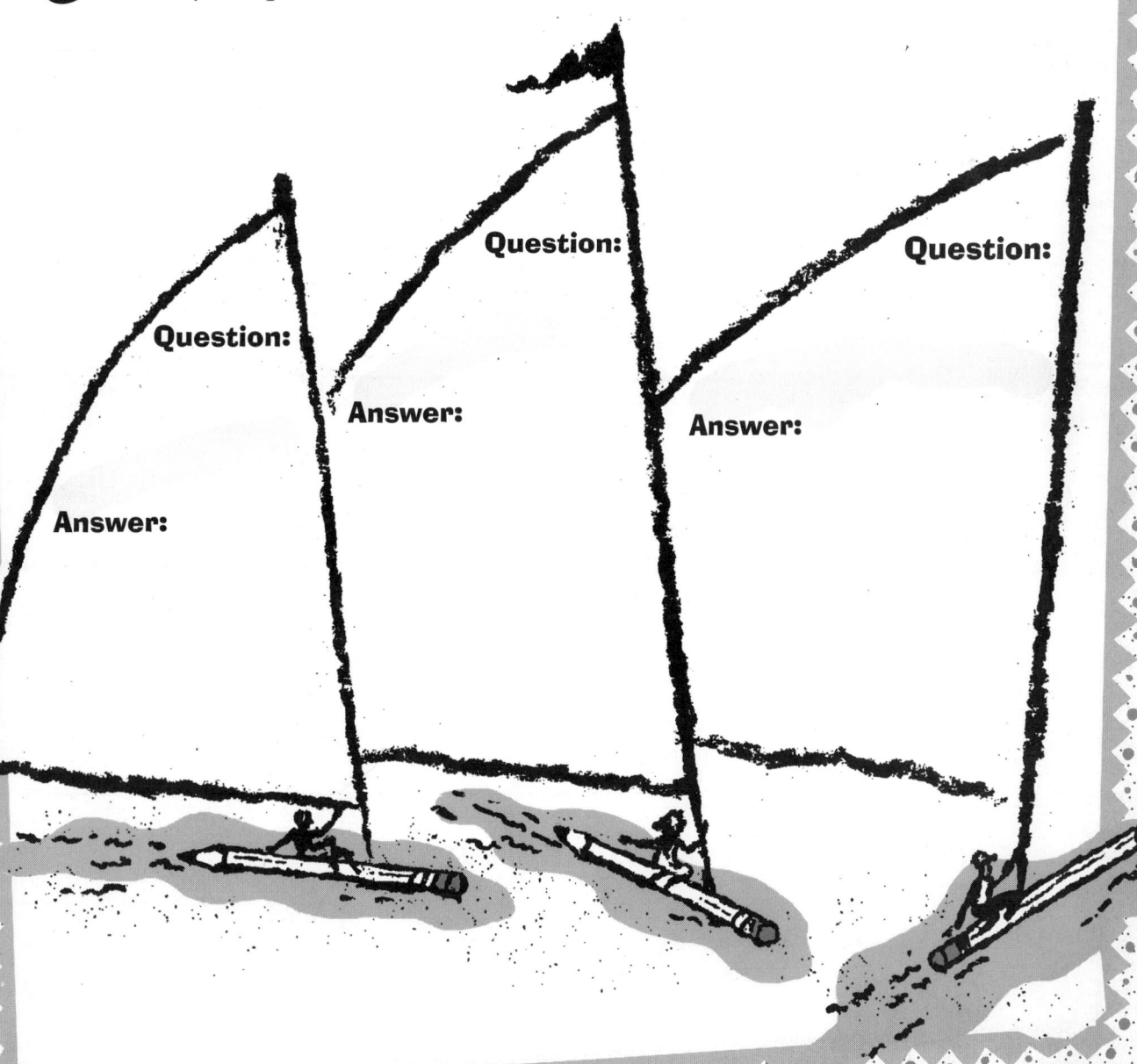

Question:

Answer:

Question:

Answer:

Question:

Answer:

Week 2

Name _____ Date _____

Word World

Most of the time you know more about a word than you think you do. A good way to find out how much you already know about a word is to make a word web.

1 Think about the word *nautical*.

2 In the ovals, write any words, phrases, or ideas that you associate with the word *nautical*.

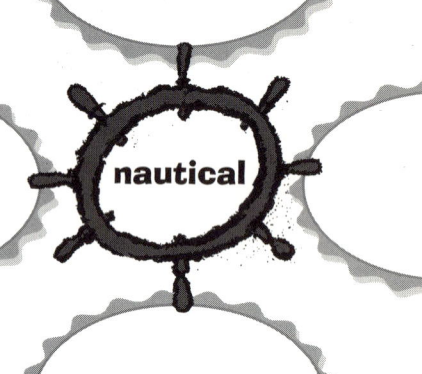

Sort It Out!

Sort the words in the word box into groups.

normal	trivial	daughter	critical	draw	caught
paw	squawk	bought	national	taught	hawk
optional		comical	crawl	fought	

Week 2

Name _____ Date _____

Plot It Out!

Plot is the events or actions in a story. A plot organizer lets you break down the features of a story such as an exposition, rising action, climax, falling action, and resolution. As you uncover each stage of the story, you will discover how the plot works. Read the story "Don't Rock the Boat" on pages 7–8 of the *Boats and Boating* magazine, and fill in the plot organizer below.

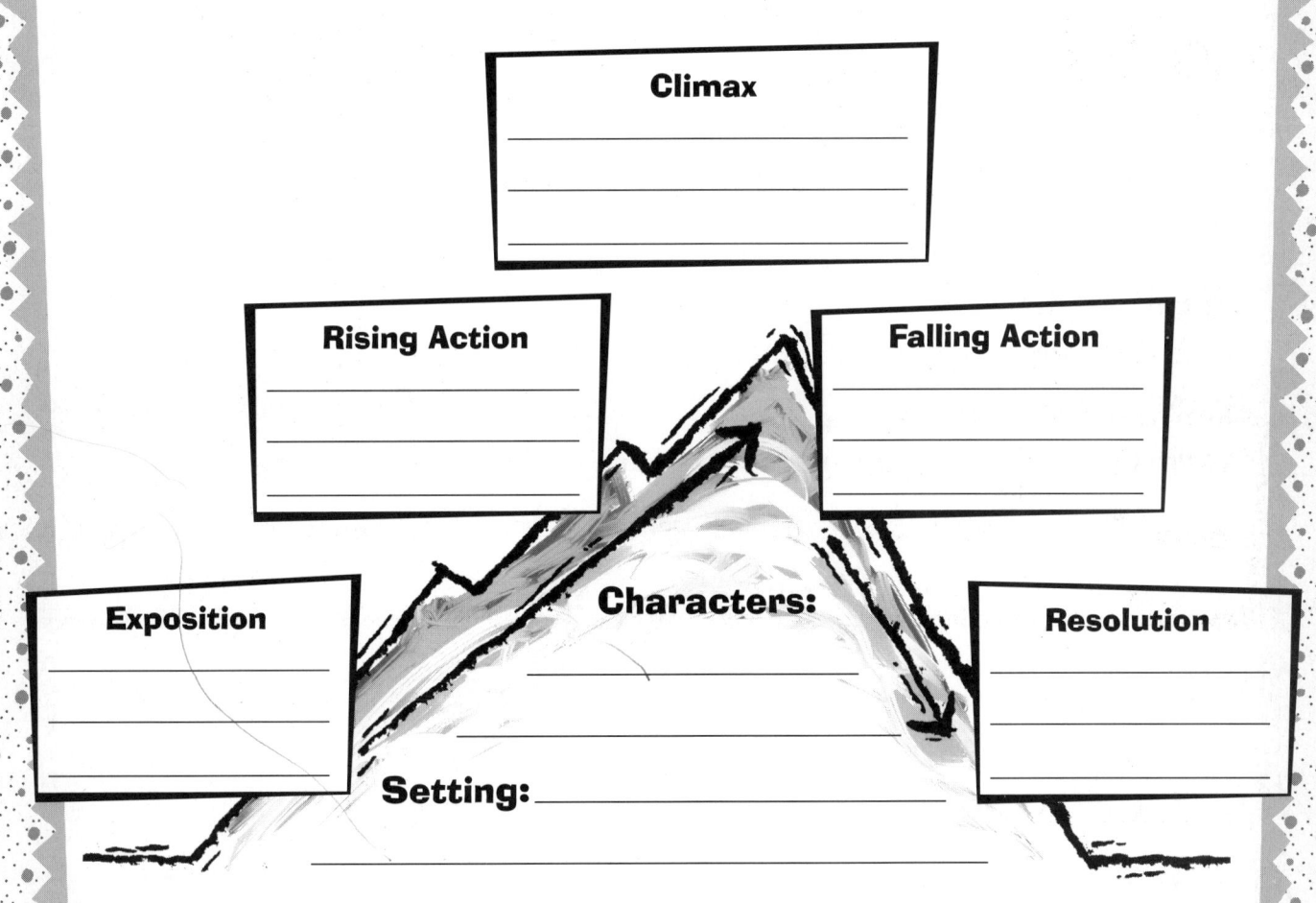

Climax
_____
_____
_____

Rising Action
_____
_____
_____

Falling Action
_____
_____
_____

Exposition
_____
_____
_____

Characters:
_____
_____

Resolution
_____
_____
_____

Setting: _____
_____

Using your imagination, think of another way the story could have ended. Write your ending on another sheet of paper.

Week 2

Name _____ Date _____

Idioms

"It's raining cats and dogs!" What does this sentence mean? Do cats and dogs fall out of the sky? The expression "It's raining cats and dogs!" is an idiom. An idiom has a special meaning as an expression that is different from the meaning of its separate words.

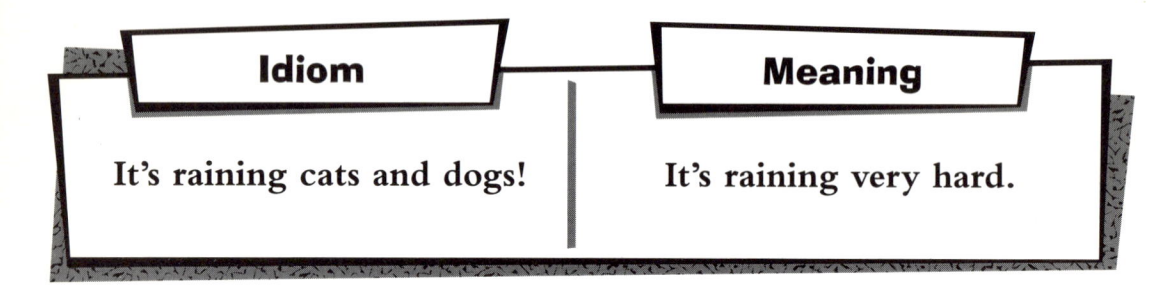

Idiom	Meaning
It's raining cats and dogs!	It's raining very hard.

Circle the letter of the answer that best tells the meaning of each idiom.

1. Heidi always <u>bends over backwards</u> to help her friends.

   a. does a handstand   **b.** refuses   **c.** does her best

2. It's best to <u>start off on the right foot</u> when you do this report.

   a. begin properly   **b.** march in a parade   **c.** walk straight

3. My big brother thinks it's funny to <u>pull my leg</u>.

   a. tug on my foot   **b.** make up a phony story   **c.** call me names

4. She <u>went out on a limb</u> to help him get the job.

   a. took a chance   **b.** climbed a tree   **c.** got lost

5. You must <u>take into account</u> what the doctor says.

   a. put in the bank   **b.** think about   **c.** forget

Week 2

Name _____ Date _____

Get Ready To Write!

A. Reflect

Read "The Submarine *Eagle:* Captain's Log" on pages 9–10 of the *Boats and Boating* magazine, and think about the questions below.

1. What are three difficult things the captain and crew deal with on the submarine?
2. How do they make their time on the submarine more fun?

B. Brainstorm

Get ready to write a journal entry about a time when you had to do something that you did not want to do. Write your thoughts below.

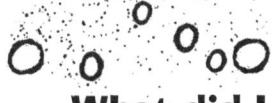

What did I have to do?	When did it happen?	Where was I?
Who was with me?	Why did I have to do it?	How did it make me feel?

Week 2

Name _____ Date _____

Time to Write

You are ready to write your own journal entry.

1. Reread what you wrote in the boxes on page 33.
2. Explain what you had to do, when you did it, who was there, and what happened.
3. In the closing sentence, tell how it made you feel.

Date _____

Dear Journal,

_____
_____
_____
_____
_____
_____
_____
_____
_____
_____
_____

Week 2

Name _____ Date _____

Summarize

1. Read the article "Chinese Dragon Boat Races" on pages 11–12 of the *Boats and Boating* magazine.

2. Identify the main point of each section and write it in the chart.

3. Skim each section of the article and find two or three details that support the main idea. Write the details in the chart.

Section Heading	Main Point	Details to Support Main Point
The Birth of a Tradition		
A Modern Celebration		

Use your notes to write a summary. The first sentence, the topic sentence, should tell what the article is about. The next sentences should provide support for the topic sentence. The last sentence should pull it all together.

_____
_____
_____
_____

Summer Success: Reading 35

Week 2

Name _____ Date _____

Self-Evaluation

1 What two things did you learn from this magazine? _____
_____
_____

2 What are two new words you learned this week? Can you use each one in a sentence?

Word	Sentence Using the Word
_____	_____
	_____
_____	_____
	_____

3 What is an idiom? _____
_____

4 What strategy do you use most often when you read? How does it help you?
_____
_____

5 What is one goal you have for next week? How will you reach it?
_____
_____
_____

Take It Home!

Magic Square

1 Select the best answer for each of the sailing terms from the numbered definitions.

2 Put the number of the definition in the proper space in the magic square box.

3 You will know that you have the magic number when the total of the numbers is the same both across and down.

Term	Definition
A. hull	1. the most important spar
B. stern	2. lines that control the sails
C. spar	3. the back of a boat
D. rigging	4. a small sailboat
E. sloop	5. a pole that holds a sail
F. schooner	6. a place where boats dock
G. marina	7. the body of the boat
H. showboat	8. a ship with entertainment
I. mainmast	9. a large, expensive sailboat

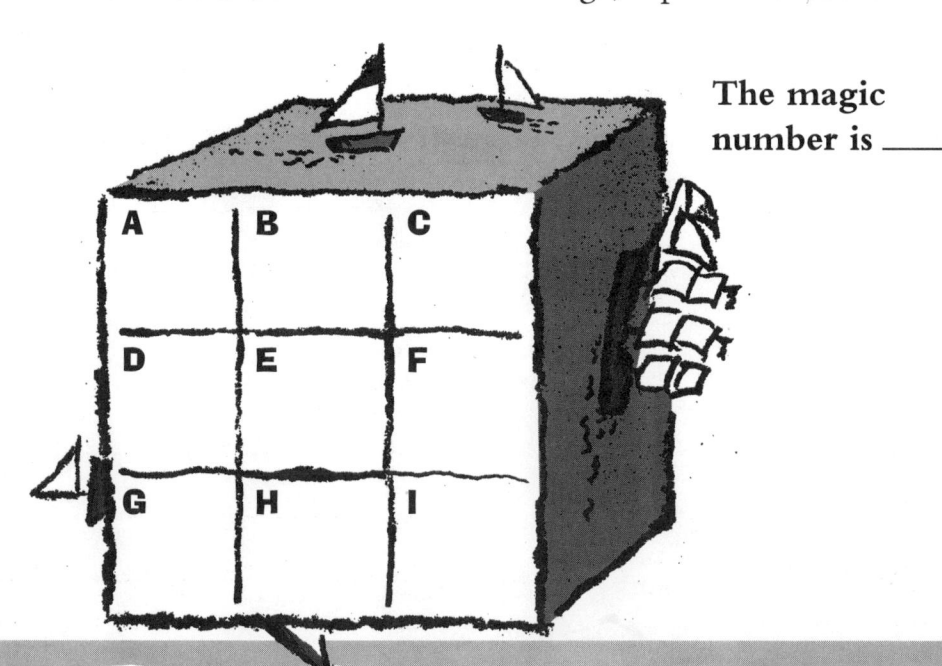

The magic number is _____ .

Summer Success: Reading 37

Take the Cake!

Don't really take the cake! An *idiom* is a combination of words that has a meaning that is different from the meaning of its separate words.

Write the word or phrase from the box on the right that could be used in place of the underlined idiom in each sentence.

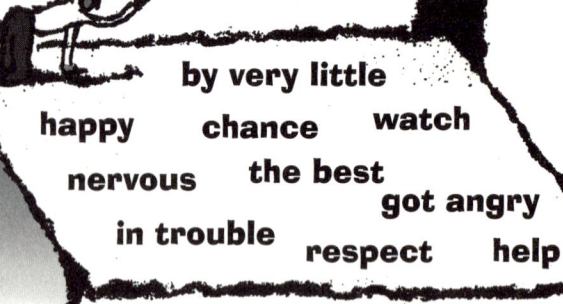

by very little
happy   chance   watch
nervous   the best
in trouble   got angry
respect   help

1 Jan had to keep an eye on her little sister. _____

2 Dad hit the roof when he saw the broken window. _____

3 I didn't have a shot in the dark at winning the race. _____

4 The new chocolate ice cream is out of this world. _____

5 I get butterflies in my stomach during spelling quizzes. _____

6 It makes me feel good to lend a hand to my mom. _____

7 Dan was in hot water for staying out late. _____

8 The little kids look up to me. _____

9 We made the train by the skin of our teeth. _____

10 When I got all A's, I was walking on air. _____

CHALLENGE: Use these three idioms in sentences of your own.

1 take the cake

2 the wrong foot

3 in one ear and out the other

Week 2 Newsletter

This week we read about different kinds of boats. We listened to a book read aloud, and we read some magazine articles and poems. Take a moment to ask your son or daughter to tell you about the book *Zia*. Also ask what he or she learned from reading and thinking about the *Boats and Boating* magazine.

The word of the week was *nautical*. The students made a word web to find out what they knew about the word *nautical*, and they sorted words related to *nautical* into groups. They also studied idioms, phrases whose meanings cannot be understood from the individual meanings of their words. "Lend an ear" is an example of an idiom. At home the students used their new knowledge of sailing terms to complete a puzzle, and they used their new knowledge of idioms to write sentences that use idioms. Ask your son or daughter to share with you the sentences he or she wrote.

Here is what your son or daughter has to say about the week:

_____
_____
_____
_____
_____
_____
_____
_____
_____
_____

Week 2 Newsletter

Learning—A Lifelong Pursuit

Learning takes place outside school, too. It happens all the time and in many different places. As a parent, you can create an atmosphere of learning for your son or daughter by providing activities and materials that encourage learning. Games can be part of the atmosphere of learning.

Games often have an educational element because they challenge students to work out solutions or come up with strategies to be successful. A lot of thinking skills are necessary to play games. Word games, and even newspaper crossword puzzles, are very useful in helping students become better thinkers and spellers. Games like chess, backgammon, and some video games require strategic higher-level thinking. Even trivia games promote making connections and recalling details.

Wouldn't You Think?

By Aileen Fisher

With so many stars
out there in space,
too many to count,
too many to trace,
wouldn't you think
a few might show
green grass growing
or tracks in snow?

I wonder if people
will ever know.

The Craft of Poetry

A poet usually has a message to tell readers. Answer these questions about the message in the poem.

1 What do you think the speaker of the poem is wondering about?
_____
_____

2 Why do you think the poet wrote the title as a question?
_____
_____

Summer Success®: Reading

Week 3

Name _____ Date _____

Before You Read

Readers bring information, ideas, and feelings to everything they read. Thinking about and gathering this knowledge helps a reader understand information.

① With a partner, discuss the term *science fiction*. What does it mean to you? What does it mean to your partner?

② Write your ideas in the word web.

③ List words, phrases, or situations you think of when you hear the term *science fiction*.

(Word web with "Science Fiction" in the center connected to four empty ovals)

Browse a Bit

Take a moment to look through the *Science Fiction* magazine.

- Look at the cover, the pictures and other graphic features, the headings of articles, story titles, and words in bold.

- Below, write any questions that you have about this magazine or the topic *science fiction*.

_____

_____

Week 3

Name _____ Date _____

Seeing the Story

When you read, do you ever imagine or "see" the story? Most of the time, authors try to help you "see" the action or events, the characters, and the setting.

1 Read "The Test" on pages 4–7 of the *Science Fiction* magazine, and notice the words that the author uses to help you see the story.

2 Fill in the storyboard to retell what happens in "The Test." Draw pictures of the action. Then explain what is happening in each picture.

What do you think Malik learned from The Test?

_____

Summer Success®: Reading 43

Week 3

Name _____ Date _____

Thinking Tree

A thinking tree is a great way to organize new information as you read. It connects main ideas and details to different "branches" to show the connections.

1. Read "Interview with a Robot" on pages 8–9 of the *Science Fiction* magazine.
2. Identify two main ideas, and write them in the organizer below.
3. Include details that support each main idea.

Title: "Interview with a Robot"

Main Idea:

Main Idea:

Details:

Details:

Draw a Conclusion

On another sheet of paper, write a paragraph about what you think would happen to the world if robots did most of the work.

44 Summer Success®: Reading

Week 3

Name _____ Date _____

Word World

The word *robotics* is made up of the root word *robot* + the suffixes *-ic* and *-s*. Write a list of the words that end with the suffix *-ic*.

Words that end with the suffix *-ic*

_____ _____ _____
_____ _____ _____
_____ _____ _____
_____ _____ _____

Add the suffix *-ist* to the underlined word in each sentence below. Use each new word to complete the sentences. Remember that you will have to make some spelling changes. For example, to add *-ist* to the word *geology*, you must drop the *y* before adding the suffix. (geologist)

1 I love the way Michael plays the piano. He is a wonderful

_____.

2 Rosa does very well in biology. She should study to be a

_____.

3 Dermatology is the study of the skin. A _____ is a doctor who studies the skin.

4 If you enjoy studying psychiatry, you should become a

_____.

5 A person who studies nutrition and can recommend a healthful diet is a

_____.

Summer Success®: Reading 45

Week 3 Name _____ Date _____

Get Ready to Write!

Gather Information

News stories answer the questions: *Who? What? When? Where? Why?* and *How?* These are called the 5 W and H questions.

Pretend you are a news reporter. You have to write a news story about a teenager from Houston, Texas, who built a robot that cleans peoples' messy rooms. Use the chart below to keep track of information for your story.

Headline: Teen Builds Robot Room Cleaner!

Who created it?

_____

What can it do?

_____

When will it be available?

_____

Where was it developed?

_____

Why is it important?

_____

How will it change the world?

_____

Closing Sentence: Write a sentence that tells whether you think this invention is a good one or a bad one and why.

46 Summer Success®: Reading

Week 3

Name _____ Date _____

Time to Write

You are ready to write your own news story.

1 First, write the headline.

2 Next, tell *who, what, when, where, why,* and *how.*

3 Write your closing sentence.

4 Reread your news story, making sure you have used correct grammar and punctuation.

Headline: _____

Week 3

Name _____ Date _____

Sort It Out!

Sort the following words into categories.

nervous   automatic   gigantic   patriotic
generous   outrageous   exposure   jealous
signature   dramatic   curious   failure   symbolic

_____ | _____ | _____

Reasons for grouping the words this way:
_____
_____
_____

Use the Clues

Write a word from the word box above that fits the clue.

1. This -*ous* word is worried. _____
2. This -*ic* word is huge. _____
3. This -*ous* word is giving. _____
4. This -*ure* word is the opposite of success. _____
5. This -*ure* word is a name. _____
6. This -*ic* word goes on its own. _____

48   Summer Success®: Reading

Week 3

Name _____ Date _____

Picture It!

1 Read the article "Fun in Space" on pages 13-14 in the *Science Fiction* magazine.

2 Select a passage from the article and draw a picture of what you see in your mind.

3 After reading the article, write the key words that helped you visualize and the connections you made to the passage.

Key Words: _____

_____

Connections I Made: _____

_____

Picture:

Compare How You Relax

Use the Venn diagram below to show how the ways you relax are similar to and different from an astronaut's.

1 In the left circle, write the ways you relax.

2 In the right circle, write the ways astronauts relax.

3 In the center, write ways that both you and astronauts relax.

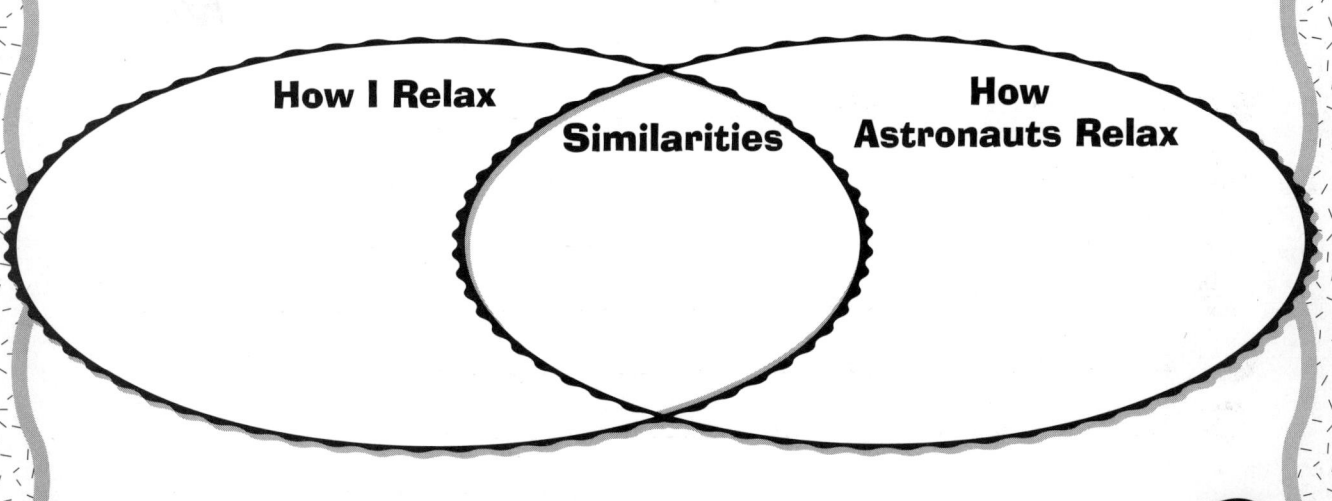

How I Relax | **Similarities** | **How Astronauts Relax**

Summer Success®: Reading 49

Week 3

Name _____ Date _____

Self-Evaluation

1 How would you describe this magazine to a friend? _____
_____
_____

2 What did you enjoy learning from this magazine? What did you like the least?
_____
_____

3 What are two new words you learned this week? Can you use each one in a sentence?

Word	Sentence Using the Word
_____	_____
	_____
_____	_____
	_____

4 Name a strategy that you used in your reading this week. How did it work?
_____
_____

5 Describe yourself as a reader. _____
_____
_____

Summer Success®: Reading

Concept Circles

Read the set of words in each circle. Complete each circle by writing the vocabulary word that relates to the other words in the circle.

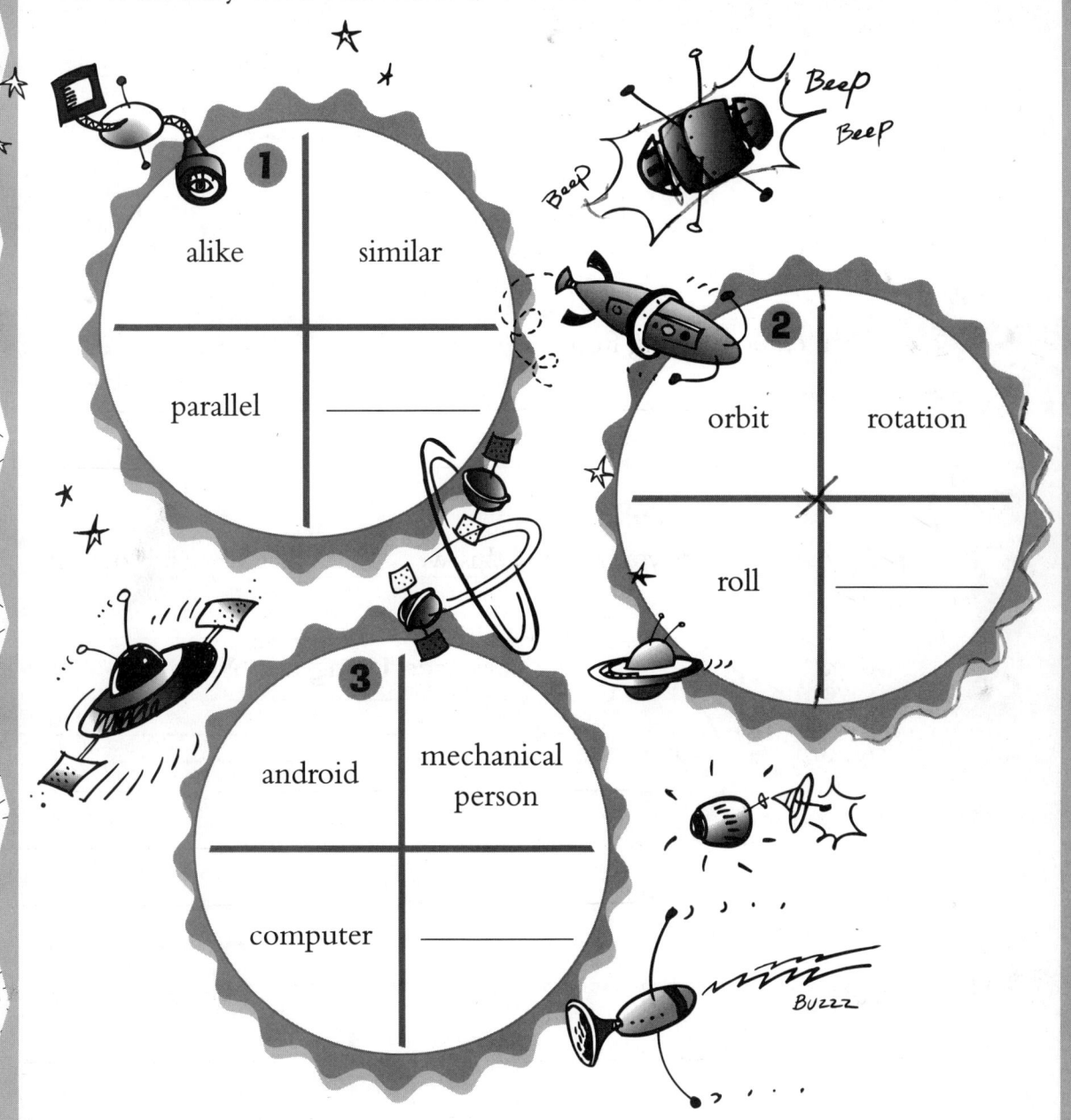

1. alike | similar | parallel | ____

2. orbit | rotation | roll | ____

3. android | mechanical person | computer | ____

CHALLENGE: On another sheet of paper, make your own concept circle for another vocabulary word that you learned this week.

How Well Do You Know Your Words?

Synonyms are two or more words that share similar meanings.
EXAMPLE: fast/quick

Antonyms are words that mean the opposite of each other.
EXAMPLE: clumsy/graceful

Words on the flying saucer: science fiction, computer, future, queasy, astronaut, cope, resembles, wilting, robot, alien, spaceship, terrestrial, discovery, revolution

Write the word from the flying saucer that answers each question.

1. Which word is a synonym for *looks like*? _____
2. Which word is an antonym for *past*? _____
3. Which word is a synonym for *flying saucer*? _____
4. Which word is a synonym for *drooping*? _____
5. Which word is a synonym for *earthly*? _____

CHALLENGE: Synonym Search
How many synonyms can you name for each word below? Write as many as you can. **HINT:** If you get stuck, check a thesaurus.

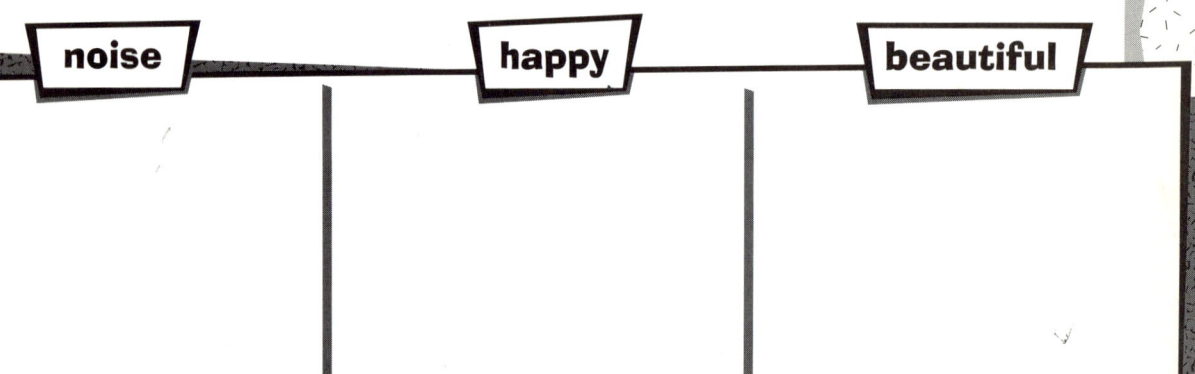

noise	happy	beautiful

Summer Success: Reading

Week 3 Newsletter

This week we read about science fiction, such as robots and future worlds. We listened to a book read aloud, read some magazine articles, and read some poems. Take a moment to have your son or daughter tell you about the book we are reading. Ask what he or she learned from reading and thinking about the *Science Fiction* magazine.

The word of the week was *robotics*. The students worked with this word to learn about the word part called a *suffix*. They made a list of words that end with the suffix -ic and sorted words according to their suffixes. Encourage your son or daughter to share the list of synonyms as well as what he or she knows about suffixes.

Here is what your son or daughter has to say about the week:

_____
_____
_____
_____
_____
_____
_____
_____
_____
_____
_____
_____
_____
_____
_____

Summer Success®: Reading

Week 3 Newsletter

The More You Read . . .

The more your son or daughter reads, the better he or she will be at reading. There are certainly plenty of science-fiction books around. Classic writers of science fiction include Arthur C. Clarke and Ray Bradbury. Listed below are books by other writers that continue the genre of science fiction that your son or daughter explored this week. Encourage him or her to read by providing suggestions of books that meet his or her interest and reading ease. For more suggestions, talk to your local librarian, or try the Book Adventure Web site (http://www.bookadventure.org/).

***The Green Book* by Jill Paton Walsh (Farrar, Straus, & Giroux, 1986)** After a worldwide disaster on planet Earth, Pattie and her family travel along with other settlers to planet Shine. Each traveler is allowed to bring one personal item. Surprisingly, the blank book that Pattie brings becomes one of the most prized possessions in the colony.

***The Keeper of the Isis Light* by Monica Hughes (Aladdin, 2000)** Olwen and her faithful robot are the only inhabitants of the planet Isis, and Olwen has grown accustomed to their simple, quiet existence. When new settlers arrive, Olwen realizes just how different she is from her counterparts on Earth. Winner of the Phoenix Award.

***The Last Book in the Universe* by Rodman Philbrick (Scholastic, 2002)** In this futuristic novel, Spaz must traverse the dreary landscape to save his sister from a fatal disease. He is accompanied by an old man named Ryter who exhorts Spaz to record his experiences in a book.

***Interstellar Pig* by William Sleator (Puffin, 1995)** Barney's neighbors introduce him to a fascinating new board game called Interstellar Pig, in which rival aliens are bent on destruction. Barney soon suspects that there is more to the game—and his neighbors—than meets the eye.

If I Can Stop One Heart from Breaking

by Emily Dickinson

If I can stop one heart from breaking,

I shall not live in vain;

If I can ease one life the aching,

Or cool one pain,

Or help one fainting robin

Unto his nest again,

I shall not live in vain.

Repetition is the use of any element of language—a sound, a word, a phrase, or a sentence—more than once. Poets use repetition for a special effect, usually to create rhythm and emphasize important ideas.

1 Circle the words or phrases that the poet repeats.

2 Identify lines that the poet repeats.

What message do you think the poet is trying to tell her readers?

_____
_____
_____
_____

Week 4   Name _____   Date _____

Write Away!

Fill in the web with examples of what you might do during your lifetime to help others. Think of what you can do for your community.

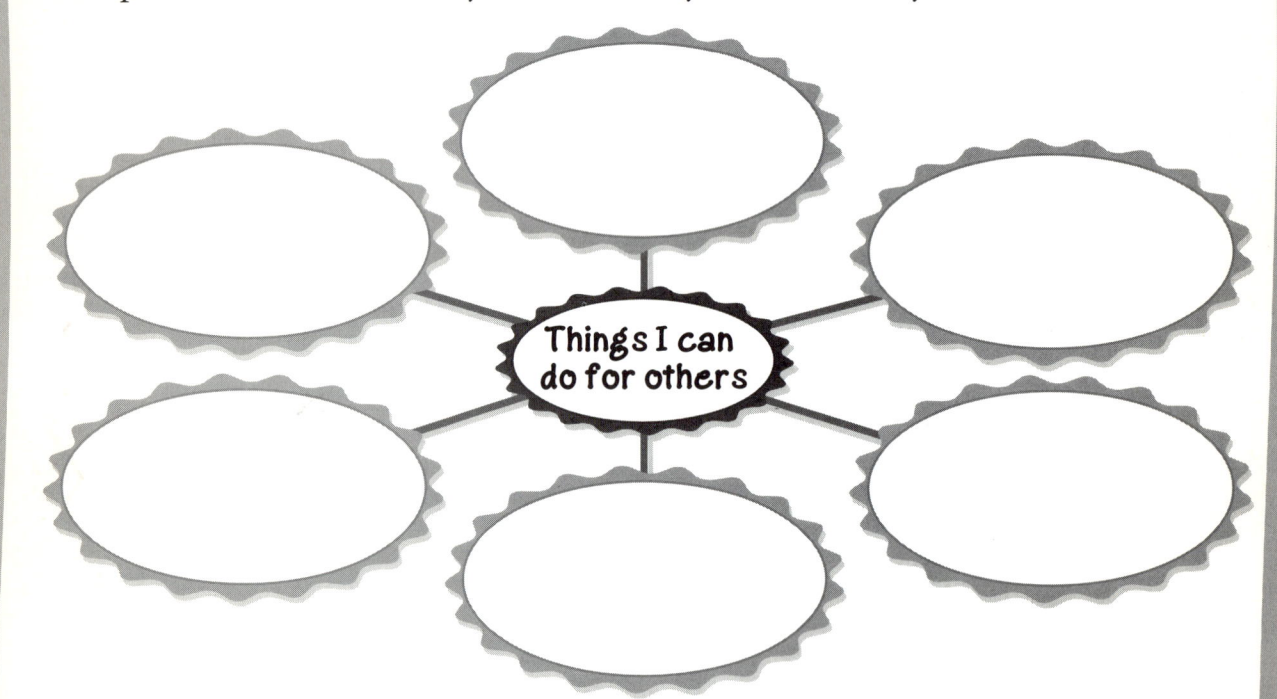

Things I can do for others

Now write your own poem inspired by "If I Can Stop One Heart from Breaking."

Title: _____

If I can...

Week 4

Name _____ Date _____

Does It "Ad" Up?

Advertisements are designed to make you want to buy a particular product. How does the ad to the right influence you? Read the ad, and then write about how it is trying to convince you to buy a product.

The new Trail Shredder makes riding more fun!

How It Influences

_____
_____
_____
_____
_____
_____
_____
_____
_____
_____
_____
_____
_____
_____
_____

Week 4

Name _____ Date _____

Connect It!

Active readers make connections when they read. How can you connect what you read to your own experiences?

❶ Read "Three People Who Changed the World" on pages 7–9 of the *They Changed Our World* magazine.

❷ Fill in the chart with examples of connections you made between the article and your own experiences.

Connections I Made	What I Learned from My Connections
To other people:	
To myself:	
To movies:	
To books:	

How does making connections help you understand what you read?

_____
_____
_____

Summer Success: Reading

Week 4

Word World

Sometimes adding a suffix can change a word to the name of a person's job or activity.

EXAMPLE: trailblaze + -er = trailblazer

Under each heading below, write words that end with the same suffix. (Each suffix means "a person who.") An example of each is provided.

-er	-ist	-ent	-ian
runner	scientist	president	musician

The missing word in each sentence below ends with one of the above suffixes. Use the clues in the sentence to figure out the word.

1. A person who does magic tricks is a _____ .
2. An athlete who swims is a _____, and one who dives is a _____ .
3. A person who resides in a town or city is a _____ .
4. Someone who studies the economy is an _____ .

Week 4

Name _____ Date _____

Sum It Up!

Follow the directions below to write a summary of the article "Beatlemania Sweeps the Nation!" on pages 10–11 of the *They Changed Our World* magazine.

1 Think about the main points in the interview. List four main points in the head outlines below.

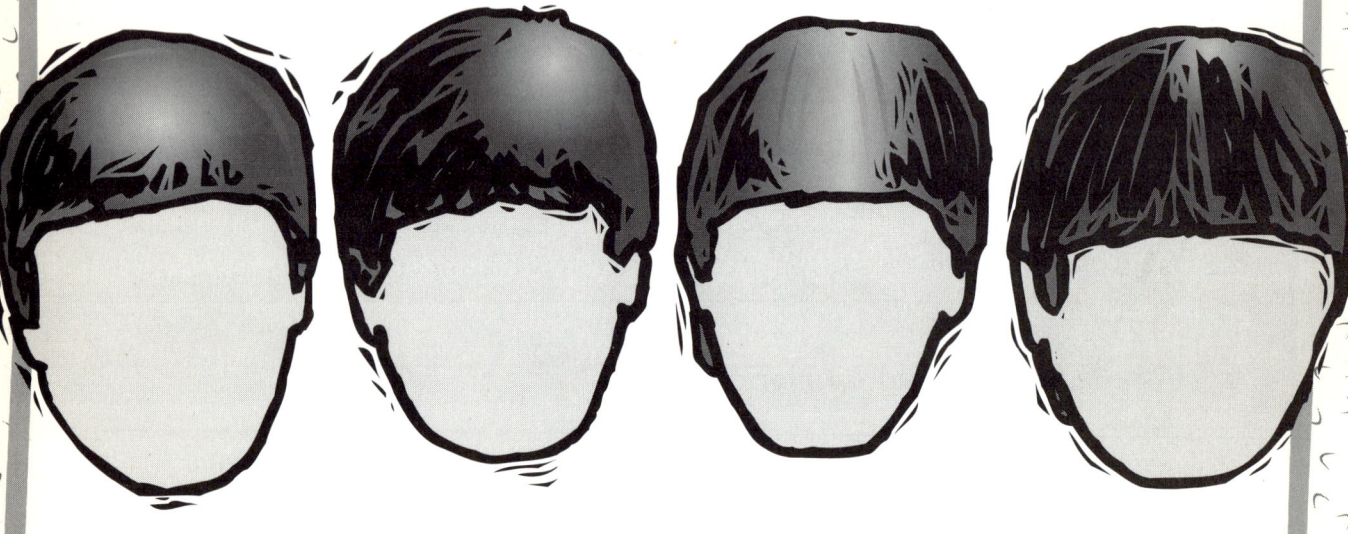

2 Next to "Main Idea Sentence," draft an opening, or lead, sentence. This should include the title and main idea of the piece you read.

3 Draft a wrap-up sentence that ties all your points together. You can restate the main idea in a different way.

4 Use your work on this page to write a summary on another sheet of paper.

Main Idea Sentence: (What is the article about? What is the message about the topic?)

_____

_____

Wrap-Up Sentence: _____

_____

_____

Homographs

Homographs are words that are spelled alike but have different meanings (table). Sometimes they are pronounced differently (bow). The meaning of a homograph can be found only from the way it is used in a sentence.

A. Write a list of homographs.

_____   _____

_____   _____

_____   _____

B. Use the context of each sentence to figure out the meaning of each underlined word.

1 The ship was bound for Florida.

Meaning _____

2 We were bound by the rules of the game.

Meaning _____

3 Nick left his keys on the counter next to the sink.

Meaning _____

4 The lawyer made a speech to counter the claims.

Meaning _____

5 A white dove is a sign of peace.

Meaning _____

6 LaKeisha dove into the pool to cool off.

Meaning _____

Week 4

Name _____ Date _____

Get Ready to Write!

Gather Ideas

1 Reread the poem "My Great Uncle" on page 15 of the *They Changed Our World* magazine.

2 Think about a person who has positively influenced your life.

3 Make a list of interesting details about that person.

What did this person do for me?

What did this person tell me?

What did I do with this person?

What do I want to say to this person?

What memories do I have about this person?

Week 4

Name _____ Date _____

Time to Write

You are ready to write your own poem about a person who has positively affected your life.

1 Write your first line. Remember that the last line will be the same.

2 Use the details you listed in the graphic organizer on page 62 to help you write the lines for your poem. Your poem does not have to rhyme.

3 Give your poem a title.

Title: _____

Week 4

Name _____ Date _____

Self-Evaluation

1 How would you describe the *They Changed Our World* magazine to a friend?
_____
_____

2 What are three facts or ideas you learned from this magazine?
_____
_____
_____

3 What are two new words you learned this week? Use each one in a sentence.

Word	Sentence Using the Word
_____	_____
	_____
_____	_____
	_____

4 What strategy do you use the most when you read? How does it help you?
_____
_____

5 Name one goal you have for next week. What can you do to reach it?
_____
_____

Take It Home!

Word Challenge

Scramble letters in the word *trailblazer* to make new words. Write your words on the lines below.

Give yourself 1 point for 3-letter words.

Give yourself 2 points for 4-letter words.

Give yourself 3 points for 5-letter words.

One has been done to get you started.

New Word	Points I Get
zebra	3

Total Points _____

Homophones

Homophones are words that sound alike but have different spellings and meanings. Homographs are words that are spelled alike but have different meanings and sometimes have different pronunciations.

Use the words below to find the homophone that fits in the sentence.

| stationary | weather | mussels | stationery | minors |
| muscles | | miners | whether | |

1 I wrote the letter on my new _____.

2 No _____ are allowed to see the movie.

3 _____ or not you make it, give me a call.

4 We feasted on _____ and clams.

Homographs

Write two sentences showing the two different meanings of the homographs below. If you can think of only one meaning, check the dictionary.

1 content

  a. _____

  b. _____

2 flight

  a. _____

  b. _____

3 second

  a. _____

  b. _____

Week 4 Newsletter

This week we read about people who have changed our world in many different ways and in many different arenas, from entertainment to exploration. We listened to a book read aloud, read some magazine articles, and read some poems. Take a moment to ask your son or daughter to tell you about the book we read aloud. Ask what he or she learned after reading and thinking about the *They Changed Our World* magazine.

The word of the week was *trailblazer*. The students made lists of words with suffixes that name people's professions. The class thought about homographs and homophones and used word meaning to determine which homophone was the correct word to use. At home, your son or daughter used the letters in the word *trailblazer* to make new words. Encourage your son or daughter to share the list of "suffix" professions as well as what he or she knows about homographs and homophones.

Here is what your son or daughter has to say about the week:

_____
_____
_____
_____
_____
_____
_____
_____
_____

Summer Success: Reading

Week 4 Newsletter

In the News

Each week the news is filled with names of people who are making a difference in the world, either positively or negatively. Encourage your son or daughter to become familiar with some of the newsmakers. Discuss how these people change our thinking and change our world.

Here are several ways to find out about people in the news:

- Read the newspaper
- Watch the news on television or listen to the radio.
- Search for Internet news sources

Use questions such as these to talk about the newsmakers:

- Why is the person in the news?
- What opinion do you have of this person?
- How might this person's actions affect you?
- What difference might this person make in the world?

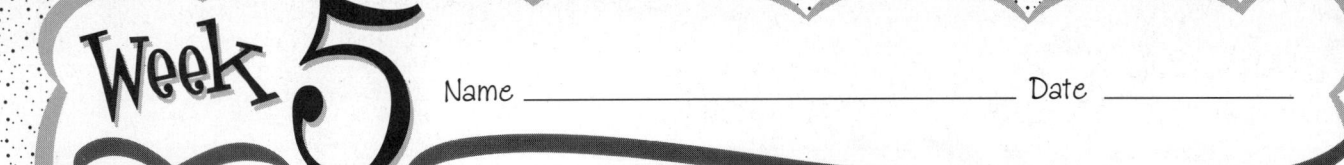

Long Trip

by Langston Hughes

The sea is a wilderness of waves,

A desert of water.

We dip and dive,

Rise and roll,

Hide and are hidden

On the sea.

Day, night,

Night, day,

The sea is a desert of waves,

A wilderness of water.

The Craft of Poetry: Metaphor

Poets sometimes describe one thing by comparing it to something else. This is called metaphor. If you forget to wear a hat out in the cold, you might say that your "ears are ice cubes." You don't mean that there are ice cubes on your head. However, by comparing your ears to ice, the metaphor shows how cold your ears feel.

1 To what is the sea being compared?
_____

2 Describe what the sea is like.
_____

Week 5

Name _____ Date _____

Before You Read

You may have questions about a topic before you read. Asking questions is a great way to begin thinking about that topic. Preview the *Adventure Seekers* magazine. Then write some questions in the chart.

Questions I Have About This Topic	Reactions (fill in after reading)

Think About It

One article or one book does not always answer all of the questions you might have about a topic.

1 Which of your questions does the magazine answer?
_____

2 What new questions does the magazine raise?
_____

3 How could you find the answers to these questions?
_____

Week 5

Name _____ Date _____

Word World

Most of the time, you know more about a word than you think you do. A good way to find out how much you already know about a word is to make a word web.

1. Think about the word *adventuresome*.
2. Write words, phrases, sentences, or ideas on the spokes of the web.

- People
- Places
- *adventuresome*
- Activities
- Words That Remind Me of *Adventuresome*

Adventuresome Words

How many words can you make by using letters from the word *adventuresome*?

Give yourself 4 points for each 4-letter word, 5 points for each 5-letter word, and so on. One word has been created for you.

New Word	Points I Get
nature	6

Total Points _____

Summer Success: Reading

Week 5

Name _____ Date _____

Storyboards

1. Read "Theseus and the Minotaur, Retold" on pages 4–6 of the *Adventure Seekers* magazine.
2. Look for three of the most important events.
3. Explain what happens in each event in the storyboard.
4. Draw a picture to illustrate each event.

Title: _____

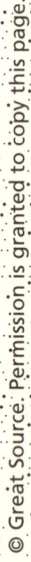

1	2	3

_____
_____

72 • Summer Success®: Reading

Week 5

Name _____ Date _____

Get Ready to Write!

Get ready to write a paragraph comparing Antarctica to the region in which you live.

A. Compare and Contrast Two Places

1 Write descriptions about the region in which you live in the left circle.

2 Write descriptions about Antarctica in the right circle.

3 Write what they have in common in the middle.

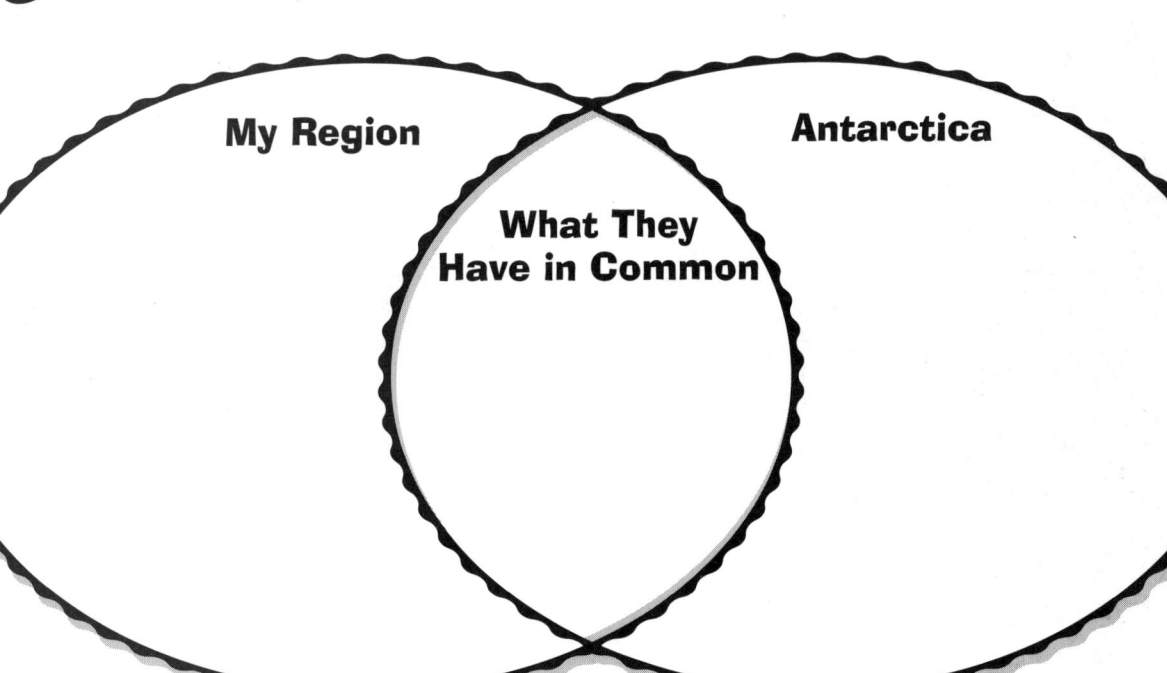

My Region | **Antarctica**

What They Have in Common

B. Write a Topic Sentence

Write a sentence that makes it clear that you are going to compare and contrast your region with Antarctica.

My topic sentence: _____
_____

Week 5

Name _____ Date _____

Time to Write

You are ready to write your own compare-and-contrast paragraph. Use what you wrote in the Venn diagram on page 73 to help you.

1 Write your topic sentence. Don't forget to indent.

2 Explain what your region has in common with Antarctica.

3 Then explain how your region and Antarctica are different.

4 Write a closing sentence that completes your paragraph.

Title: _____

Week 5

Name _____ Date _____

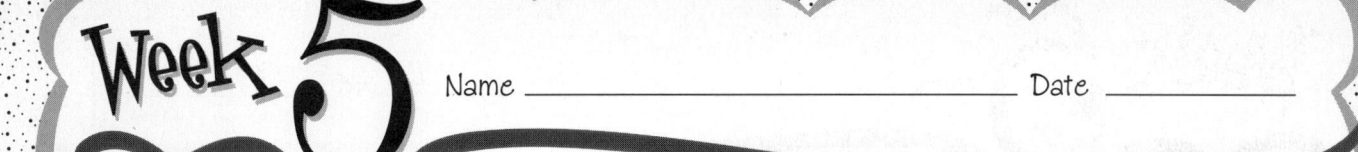

Acrobatic Analogies!

An analogy compares word pairs that are related in some way.

EXAMPLE: Cactus is to spine as rose is to ____ .
   a. nail   **b.** thorn   **c.** leaf

A good way to solve an analogy is to place the words in a sentence that shows their relationship to one another. The first pair of words can be put in this sentence: *A cactus has a prickly spine on its stem.* The second pair of words can be put in this similar sentence: *A rose has a prickly thorn on its stem.* The answer is b. thorn.

Select the word that completes each analogy.

1. Adventure is to adventuresome as tire is to ____ .

   a. sometime   **b.** tiresome   **c.** tiredness

2. Carrot is to vegetable as orange is to ____ .

   a. eat   **b.** grapefruit   **c.** fruit

3. Calculator is to add as ruler is to ____ .

   a. yardstick   **b.** measure   **c.** inches

4. Fork is to utensil as hammer is to ____ .

   a. tool   **b.** saw   **c.** nail

5. Day is to week as week is to ____ .

   a. minute   **b.** hour   **c.** month

6. Flower is to bouquet as bead is to ____ .

   a. jewelry   **b.** necklace   **c.** roses

7. Adventurous is to brave as exhausted is to ____ .

   a. tired   **b.** exhaust   **c.** lively

Week 5

Name _____ Date _____

Sum It Up!

When you look at an article, notice how the author organizes the information into sections with headings. Think about the main point of each section. When you put together the main points, you will have a summary of the article.

1 Reread the article "Riding the Russian Mountain" on pages 9–11 of the *Adventure Seekers* magazine.

2 Stop after each bold heading and think about the main point of the section. Write each main point in the chart.

3 Then write a main idea sentence and a closing sentence.

4 Write your paragraph on another sheet of paper.

Title: _____

Main Point: _____

Main Point: _____

Main Point: _____

Main Point: _____

Main Idea Sentence (What is the whole piece about?):

Wrap-up Sentence (Tie main points together/restate main idea.):

76 Summer Success® Reading

Week 5

Name _____ Date _____

Connect It!

Read "Two Views from the Mountain" on pages 12–14 of the *Adventure Seekers* magazine. As you read, try to make connections to adventure seekers or events in the articles. Can you make connections to your own experiences? Can you make connections to the experiences of others you know?

Connections I Made	What I Learned from My Connections
To my life:	
To my friends and family:	
To other athletes:	
To other selections:	

Retell It!

Choose a section from one of the articles and write a retelling of that section. Describe the main events in the order in which they happened. Write your retelling on another sheet of paper.

Summer Success®: Reading

Week 5

Name _____ Date _____

Self-Evaluation

1 How would you describe to a friend what this magazine was about?
_____
_____

2 What are two new facts you learned from this magazine?
_____
_____

3 What are two new words you learned this week? Use each one in a sentence.

Word	Sentence Using the Word
_____	_____
_____	_____

4 What strategy do you find most helpful? When do you use it?
_____
_____

5 List one goal you have for next week. What will you do to reach that goal?
_____
_____

Take It Home!

Write "SOME" Words

The word *adventuresome* is made up of the root word *adventure* and the suffix *-some*, which means "full of." Write as many words as you can that end with the suffix *–some*. Write them on the lines below.

Looking closely at a new word can make you think of other words that are related to the new word. The following words contain the root word *adventure*. Think of what you already know about suffixes and prefixes to predict the meaning of each word. Then check the meaning and part of speech in the dictionary.

	Word	How It Is Related to *Adventure*	Dictionary Meaning & Part of Speech
1	adventurous		
2	misadventure		
3	adventurer		
4	adventures		
5	adventured		
6	adventuring		

Summer Success: Reading

Eponyms

Eponyms are words that come from the names of people, places, or institutions. Some words that we use every day are eponyms.

EXAMPLE: The day of the week, Thursday, comes from the Norse god of thunder, Thor.

Match the eponym with the word it comes from.

Eponym

1. Rubik's cube
2. bloomers
3. pasteurize
4. ritzy
5. January
6. volcano
7. sandwich
8. teddy bear
9. hamburger
10. saxophone
11. tuxedo
12. sideburns
13. lima bean
14. chihuahua
15. Brussels sprouts

Word

A. Janus (god of beginnings and endings)
B. C. Ritz—fancy hotel operator
C. Amelia Bloomer, feminist
D. Vulcan, Roman god of fire
E. Theodore Roosevelt, president
F. Louis Pasteur, a scientist
G. Brussels, Belgium
H. Tuxedo Park, New York
I. Earl of Sandwich, a nobleman
J. Lima, Peru
K. Chihuahua, Mexico
L. Hamburg, Germany
M. Anton Sax, Belgian instrument maker
N. E. Rubik, inventor
O. Ambrose Burnside, Civil War general

Week 5 Newsletter

This week we read the *Adventure Seekers* magazine and explored topics such as dancers who use the mountains as their stage. We also read about adventure seekers who explored Antarctica and climbed Mt. Everest. We listened to a book read aloud, read some magazine articles, and read some poems. Ask your son or daughter what he or she learned after reading and thinking about the *Adventure Seekers* magazine.

The word of the week was *adventuresome*. The students made connections to the word *adventuresome* and learned about the suffix *-some*, which means "full of." At home, they examined the word *adventuresome* further and determined the meanings of other words that share the same root word. They also worked with analogies, puzzling out how pairs of words are related to one another. Encourage your son or daughter to share with you his or her analogies as well as the list of eponyms.

Here is what your son or daughter has to say about the week:

_____
_____
_____
_____
_____
_____
_____
_____

Week 5 Newsletter

Armchair Adventure

Pursuing any kind of adventure, especially one for the first time, involves some risk. One way to minimize the risk is to learn as much as possible about the activity. If your son or daughter aspires to climb a mountain or travel to a faraway land, he or she should do some research at the library, at a bookstore, or on the Internet.

For those students who prefer to experience their adventures from the comfort of home, suggest that they check out one or more of the titles below.

***Crocodiles, Camels & Dugout Canoes* by Bo Zaunders (Dutton, 1998)** A collection of articles describing eight adventurous episodes that take place in various parts of the world. Most of these true-life adventures are about survival in remote, isolated locales.

***Jumping the Nail* by Eve Bunting (Harcout, 1991)** In a coastal California community, a group of teenagers are drawn to the "Nail," a seaside cliff where they challenge one another to dive into the water. Dru's troubled friend Elisa is pulled into the crowd by peer pressure, and now it is up to Dru to stop Elisa before the game goes too far.

***My Side of the Mountain* by Jean Craighead George (Puffin, 2001)** Sam Gribbley runs away from his family in New York City to live alone in the Catskill Mountains. Over the course of a year, he has many adventures, including encounters with wild animals, but ultimately he realizes that he needs human companionship.

***The River* by Gary Paulsen (Bantam, 1998)** A man is accompanied by a government psychologist on a survival mission into the wilderness. Although their mission is considered an experiment of sorts, it becomes a life-and-death matter when a freak storm hits.

***Wings* by Jane Yolen (Harcourt Brace Jovanovich, 1997)** A picture book about the Greek myth of Icarus and his father Daedalus, who tried to escape their imprisonment on the island of Crete. The father fashioned pairs of wings for them and warned his son not to fly too close to the sun.

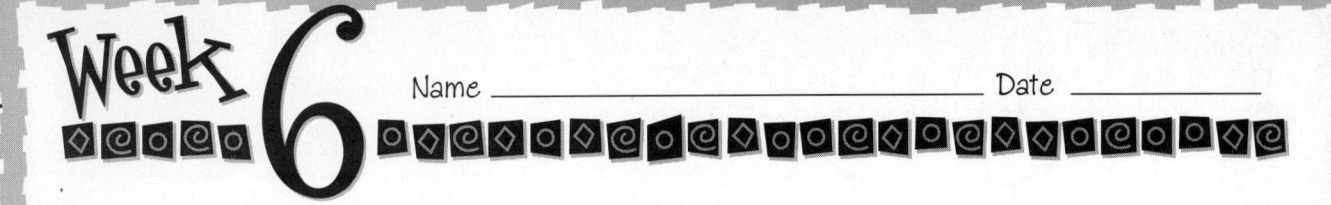

What Is It That Upsets the Volcanoes

by Pablo Neruda

translated *by William O'Daly*

What is it that upsets the volcanoes
that spit fire, cold and rage?

Why wasn't Christopher Columbus able to discover Spain?

How many questions does a cat have?

Do tears not yet spilled
wait in small lakes?

Or are they invisible rivers
that run toward sadness?

Make a Connection

What does this poem make you wonder about?

1. _____
2. _____
3. _____

Week 6

Name _____ Date _____

Before You Read

Previewing prepares you for a selection that you are about to read. It gives you a chance to connect to the topic before you begin.

1 Read the introduction to the *Natural Disasters* magazine on page 3.

2 Look at the features such as photos, selection titles, and words in bold. What do they suggest the magazine will be about?

3 Answer the questions below.

What is this magazine about?

_____
_____
_____

What questions do you have about this magazine?

_____
_____
_____

If you could add your own drawing to the art in this magazine, what would you draw? Sketch your picture in the space provided. Then, write a caption describing your picture.

My Art

My caption: _____
_____
_____

84 Summer Success®: Reading

Week 6

Name _____ Date _____

Word World

Most of the time, you know more about a word than you think you do. A good way to find out how much you already know about a word is to make a word web.

1 Think about the word *catastrophe*.

2 Write words, phrases, sentences, or ideas on the spokes of the web.

3 If you need to, add your own lines.

catastrophe

CHALLENGE Brainstorm a list of the words you can make from the word *catastrophe*. Organize the words in two columns: one-syllable words and two-syllable words. One word in each column has been provided for you.

One-syllable Words	Two-syllable Words
start	carpet

Summer Success®: Reading 85

Week 6

Name _____ Date _____

Plot It Out!

Most stories are organized in the same way. This helps you, the reader, know what to expect. Fill in the plot organizer below with events from "The House on Dogwood Lane," on pages 4-6 of the *Natural Disasters* magazine.

Title: _____

Climax
_____
_____
_____

Rising Action
_____
_____
_____

Falling Action
_____
_____
_____

Exposition
_____
_____
_____

Characters:
_____
_____

Resolution
_____
_____
_____

Setting: _____

86 Summer Success®: Reading

Week 6

Name _____ Date _____

Get Ready to Write a Summary!

Reread "Preparing for an Earthquake" on pages 7-9 of the *Natural Disasters* magazine. As you read, think about the main points of the article. Use the chart below to organize your ideas.

Brainstorm

List 4–5 main points.

_____
_____
_____
_____
_____

Organize

Now write a lead sentence: (What is the whole article about?)
_____
_____

Reread your list of 4-5 main points. Turn each point into a sentence, and write the sentences in time order below.

Main-point sentences: _____
_____
_____
_____
_____

Wrap-up sentence:
_____

Summer Success®: Reading   87

Week 6

Name _____ Date _____

Time to Write

You are ready to write your own summary about preparing for an earthquake. Use the notes from page 87 to help you write your summary.

1 Begin with your lead sentence.

2 Then, in your own words, write the sentences that tell the main points of the article.

3 Write a wrap-up sentence that ties all of your points together.
Hint: You can restate the main idea in a different way.

Title: _____

88 Summer Success®: Reading

Week 6

Name _____ Date _____

Synonyms and Antonyms

A list of synonyms and antonyms follows each boldfaced word below. Sort the synonyms from the antonyms, and write each word in the correct column. Use a dictionary or a thesaurus to check your answers. The first list has been done for you.

Words	Synonyms	Antonyms
final beginning, end, first, last, outset, starting, terminal, ultimate	end last terminal ultimate	beginning first outset starting
1 accurate correct, exact, false, incorrect, right, true, untrue, wrong		
2 enthusiastic bored, dejected, eager, excited, happy, inactive, spirited, tired		
3 poised awkward, balanced, clumsy, coordinated, dignified, gangling, graceful		

Summer Success®: Reading

Week 6

Name _____ Date _____

Understand It!

A thinking tree is a great way to organize new information as you read. It connects main ideas and details into different "branches" and helps you see the connections.

1 Read "Hurricane Havoc" on pages 10-11 of the *Natural Disasters* magazine.

2 Write each main idea on one of the lines provided. **Hint:** Look at the bold headings in the selection.

3 Write supporting details on the lines provided below each main idea line.

Title: _____

Main Idea: _____

Details

Details

Main Idea: _____

Details

Details

Main Idea: _____

Details

Details

Describe what you know:

On another sheet of paper, write a description of a hurricane, using the main ideas and details you listed in the thinking tree.

90 Summer Success®: Reading

Week 6

Name _____ Date _____

Monitor Your Understanding

It is important to understand what you read. It is also important to be aware of any questions that you have about the topic as well as any information that you do not understand.

Before You Read
Before you read "Mount St. Helens: Story of a Volcano" on pages 12-14 of the *Natural Disasters* magazine, answer these questions:

1. What do I know about volcanoes? _____
_____

2. What questions do I have about volcanoes? _____
_____

During Reading
As you read the article, try to clarify what you understand by rereading, retelling, and asking questions.

_____
_____
_____
_____

After Reading
What did I learn about volcanoes?

_____
_____
_____

Where could I look to find more information?

_____
_____

Summer Success®: Reading

Week 6

Name _____ Date _____

Self-Evaluation

1 How would you describe to a friend what this magazine is about?

_____
_____

2 What are two new facts you learned from this magazine?

_____
_____

3 What are two new words you learned this week? Use each one in a sentence.

Word	Sentence Using the Word
_____	_____
	_____
_____	_____
	_____

4 What strategy did you use in your reading this week? How did it work?

_____
_____

5 Describe yourself as a reader.

_____
_____

92 Summer Success®: Reading

Take It Home!

Use the word box to help you build words that start with the prefix *re-*. The prefix *re-* means "again," as in the word *redo,* which means "to do again."

After you have formed your words, write your own definition for each word. When you finish, check a dictionary to see whether your definitions are correct.

Prefix + Word	Definition

CHALLENGE: On another sheet of paper, list all the words that you can think of that contain the prefix *re-*.

Think of the words you have been studying while reading the *Natural Disasters* magazine. One word completes each sentence below. Complete the word that goes with the sentence.

1. The teacher needed an __ c __ __ r __ __ __ count of students who were ordering hot lunches.

2. The plane dove in a __ __ i __ __ l , spinning to the ground.

3. The volcano spit out hot, __ o __ __ __ n lava.

4. We aren't __ __ t __ __ s __ __ s __ __ about going to the movie. We'd rather play outside.

5. The firefighter made everyone __ __ a __ __ a __ __ the burning building.

6. We watched as the smoke __ __ l __ __ w __ __ up into the air like a balloon.

Acronym Acrobatics

An acronym is a shortened form of two or more words. Acronyms are usually pronounced as single words. Match the acronyms below with the words they come from.

1. SCUBA   a. personal identification number

2. RADAR   b. light amplification by stimulated emission of radiation

3. LASER   c. National Aeronautics and Space Administration

4. PIN   d. radio detection and ranging

5. NASA   e. self-contained underwater breathing apparatus

Week 6 Newsletter

This week we read about disasters and explored topics such as earthquakes and hurricanes. We also read about volcanoes and the destruction they can cause. We listened to a book read aloud, read some magazine articles, and enjoyed some poems. Take a moment to have your son or daughter tell you about the book we are reading. Ask what he or she learned from reading and thinking about the *Natural Disasters* magazine.

The word of the week was *catastrophe*. The class members made a word web using the word *catastrophe* and explored what they already knew about the word. Students studied synonyms and antonyms, and they examined the relationships between these words. Encourage your son or daughter to share with you what he or she has written and has learned about disasters.

Here is what your son or daughter has to say about the week:

_____
_____
_____
_____
_____
_____
_____
_____
_____
_____
_____
_____
_____
_____

Summer Success®: Reading

Week 6 Newsletter

Always Be Prepared

One of the articles that students read this week was about being prepared for an earthquake. If you live in an area that has frequent earthquakes, you are well versed in how to prepare for earthquakes. People in Florida or North Dakota, the states with the fewest number of earthquakes, might not be as well prepared for an earthquake but might, indeed, be ready for a hurricane or a tornado.

No matter where you live, it pays to be prepared. Here are some steps that you and your son or daughter can take to make your household ready for an emergency.

1. Keep a list of emergency phone numbers next to each phone in the house and/or put police and fire numbers on speed dial. As you know, calling 911 will serve you well in an emergency. Include the number of trusted (and nearby) adults who can be contacted if there are no adults at home at the time of the emergency.

2. Stock or purchase a first-aid kit.

3. Check the battery supply for radios and light sources in case of a power outage.

4. Purchase a few days' worth of nonperishable food and water supplies.

5. Make an evacuation plan in case of fire. Decide on a place to meet or a neighbor to contact to make sure everyone is accounted for.